Zodiac Signs

TAURUS

by Elizabeth Andrews

DiscoverRoo
An Imprint of Pop!
popbooksonline.com

WELCOME TO DiscoverRoo!

This book is filled with videos, puzzles, games, and more! Scan the QR codes* while you read, or visit the website below to make this book pop.

popbooksonline.com/taurus

abdobooks.com
Published by Pop!, a division of ABDO, PO Box 398166, Minneapolis, Minnesota 55439.

Printed in the United States of America, North Mankato, Minnesota.
042025
082025

THIS BOOK CONTAINS RECYCLED MATERIALS

Cover Photo: Splendoura Prints; Shutterstock Images
Interior Photos: Getty Images; Shutterstock Images; Wikimedia Commons
Editor: Tyler Gieseke
Series Designer: Laura Graphenteen

Library of Congress Control Number: 2024948386

Publisher's Cataloging-in-Publication Data
Names: Andrews, Elizabeth, author.
Title: Taurus / by Elizabeth Andrews
Description: Minneapolis, Minnesota : Pop!, 2026 | Series: Zodiac signs | Includes online resources and index
Identifiers: ISBN 9781098247966 (lib. bdg.) | ISBN 9781098248505 (ebook)
Subjects: LCSH: Taurus (Astrology)--Juvenile literature. | Bull (Astrology)--Juvenile literature. | Zodiac--Juvenile literature. | Astrology--Juvenile literature. | Astrology--Charts, diagrams, etc.--Juvenile literature.
Classification: DDC 133.52--dc23

*Scanning QR codes requires a web-enabled smart device with a QR code reader app and a camera.

TABLE OF CONTENTS

CHAPTER 1

MEET THE TAURUS!

Taurus is the second zodiac sign. People born between April 20 and May 20 are Taureans. When people ask for your "star sign," they are likely asking for your sun sign. This is the zodiac sign the sun appeared in at your birth.

WATCH A VIDEO HERE!

Violet

April 20–May 20

TAURUS

ZODIAC CALENDAR

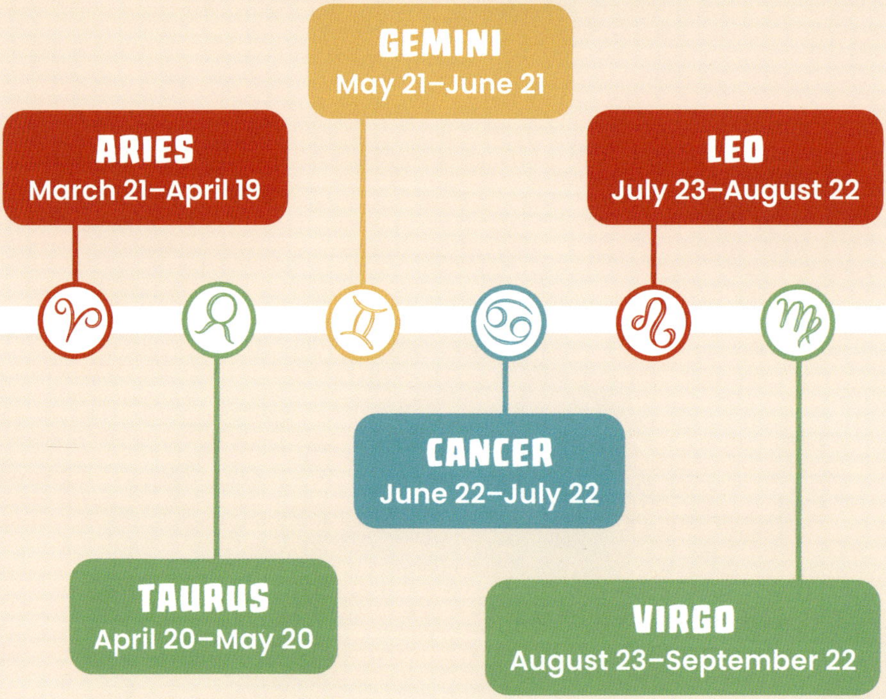

Three features help describe zodiac signs. Signs can be masculine or feminine. Each zodiac sign is given a mode. The three modes are cardinal, fixed, and mutable. Each zodiac is also

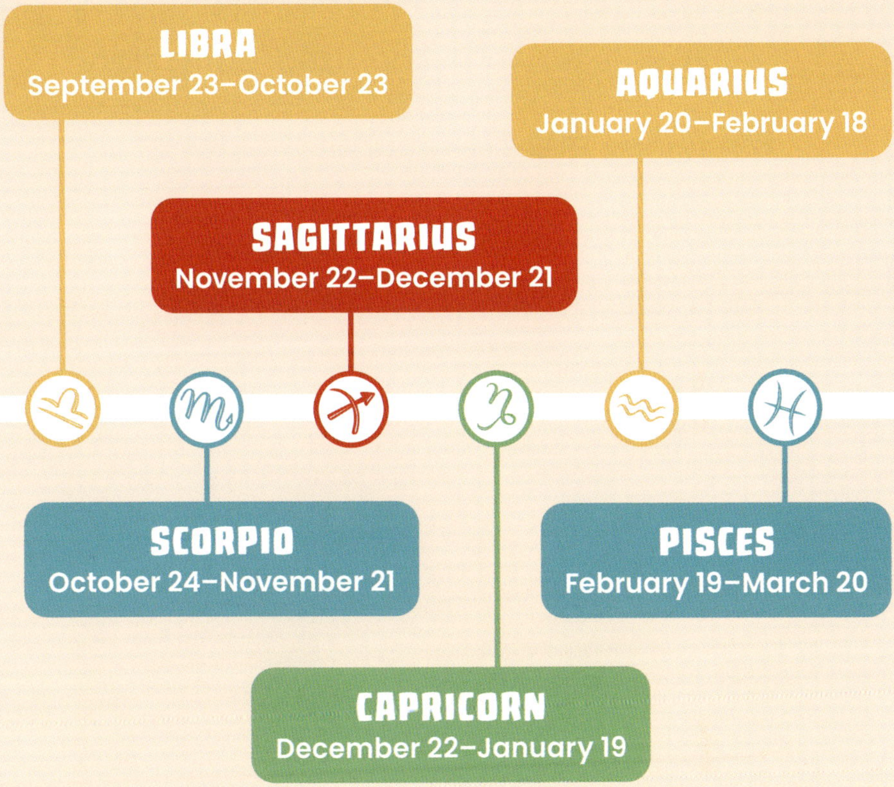

a fire, air, earth, or water sign. No zodiac signs share the same three features.

DID YOU KNOW?

Fixed signs are born in the middle of seasons.

Taurus is a feminine, fixed, earth sign. Feminine signs are grounded. Many of their actions are done **internally**. They are in touch with their own emotions and those around them.

Meditating is a grounding activity that Taureans may enjoy. It involves focusing on one's breath.

Modes describe how signs interact with the outside world. Fixed signs are very grounded. This means that they are emotionally stable and clear thinkers. They don't like change. Earth is the slowest-moving element. Earth signs are often dependable people with lots of plans. They are steady and calm.

Bulls are strong and often calm animals.

The Taurus constellation is visible from fall to spring in the Northern Hemisphere and spring to fall in the Southern Hemisphere.

Taurus is **represented** by a bull. Bulls are slow to anger and move. They are usually gentle. But they can get angry.

The ancient Greeks connected the Taurus **constellation** with Zeus, who turned into a bull to attract a woman. Other ancient people believed the constellation represented the bull that the hero Gilgamesh battled.

Zeus and the woman were pictured on coins in ancient Greece.

CHAPTER 2

HISTORY OF ASTROLOGY

Humans have looked for life's **spiritual** meaning since the beginning of time. They often looked to the stars for this. Astrology is the practice of reading the movements of planets and other **celestial** bodies and connecting them to life on Earth.

LEARN MORE HERE!

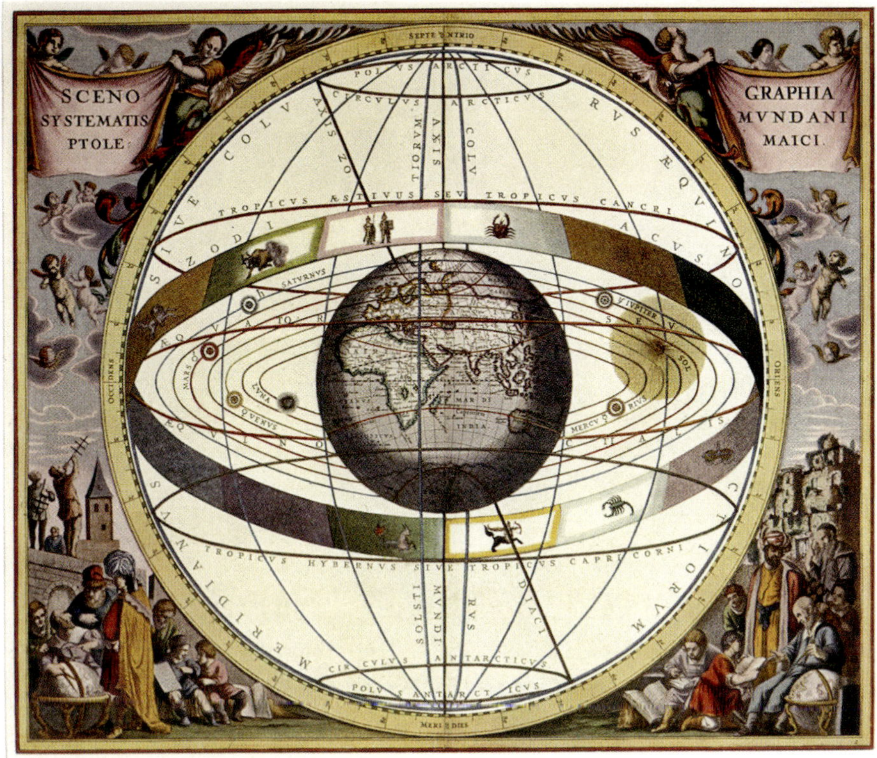

Some ancient people used the zodiac signs to predict future events.

Babylonians invented the zodiac in Mesopotamia over 5,000 years ago. Mesopotamia was the first known civilization. Babylon was one of the region's largest cities.

Ptolemy was an Egyptian man who studied the stars.

Earth and our solar system are in the Milky Way galaxy.

The zodiac is a belt of space around Earth that has 12 well-known **constellations**. Ancient people noticed that the sun seemed to move in front of these constellations throughout a year. The sun spends about a month in each constellation.

The constellations in the zodiac belt are Aries, Taurus, Gemini, Cancer, Leo, Virgo, Libra, Scorpius, Sagittarius, Capricornus, Aquarius, and Pisces. Together they make up the 12 zodiac signs. They are all **represented** by different **symbols**.

Islamic astrologers created new ways to map and measure stars.

THE ZODIAC WHEEL

DID YOU KNOW?

Most zodiac symbols are animals. The ancient Greeks called the belt of space *zodiakos kyklos,* or "circle of animals."

CHAPTER 3

HAPPIEST AT HOME

Taureans are ruled by the planet Venus. The planet is named after the Roman goddess of love, beauty, pleasure, emotions, and art. Because of this, Venus is known as a very feminine planet. Taureans love beautiful, **luxurious** things. They are also dependable and caring.

EXPLORE LINKS HERE!

Taureans enjoy nice vacations that make them feel special.

Taureans are down to earth. They find joy in the simple moments from the world around them.

Taureans may find interesting ways to show off their collections.

Taurus is a sign of property and money. Taureans' connection to Venus gives them a deep respect for beautiful things. They believe things are for enjoying. They are often collectors. Because they prize the finer things, Taureans can be **jealous** of what others have.

Taureans do not like to try new things. They prefer to go places they have already been and do things they have already done. If they try something new, they like to gather information beforehand. They are happy to share their own knowledge of places and things.

Taureans might find comfort in trying new things if they are with people they trust.

Taureans' favorite people are those who make them feel safe.

As a fixed sign, Taureans are uncomfortable with change. Sudden changes may make them angry. They may also be stubborn and refuse to change themselves. Taureans are happiest at home with their favorite people, surrounded by the things they love. No sign knows how to relax quite like a Taurus.

DID YOU KNOW?

Any quick changes to a Taurean's life will cause stress and concern. Taureans like to know what is coming.

CHAPTER 4

A SLOW SIGN

Taureans' deepest wish is to build something lasting for themselves. This could be a relationship, job, or home. Like the bull, Taureans will move slowly and surely toward their purpose. People born in the sign of Taurus are known for their drive to continue.

The emerald is the stone of love and growth.

COMPLETE AN ACTIVITY HERE!

Catherine the Great of Russia was a Taurus. She did a lot of good things for her country. She was also known for her love of fancy things.

Taureans delight in art and music. They also have an eye for the arts. They would do well in a creative job where they can take charge. People born in Taurus might find themselves working as

Taureans would be good fashion designers.

Museum curators choose art to go on display.

buyers of fashion or physical art. They are workers and leaders who can be counted on. Once Taureans find a job they love, they are likely to stay for a long time.

DID YOU KNOW?

Taureans are known for holding **grudges**.

Sabrina Carpenter is a Taurus. She writes songs about all of her feelings.

Friends of Taureans love how dependable they are. Taureans take a while to open up to new people. Once they do, though, they are giving and loving friends.

However, like the bull, Taureans can get angry. It doesn't happen often, but if they are pushed, they fight back. They can also be stubborn and have strong opinions.

Today, astrology can answer questions about an individual. People use astrology to understand who they are and why they might do what they do. It can also help people understand others in their life. A zodiac sign can point out personal skills, possibilities, and **internal motivations**.

WHAT IS A BIRTH CHART?

Each person's birth chart contains all the planets in our solar system, the moon, and the sun. The location of where each **celestial** body was based on the exact time and location of a person's birth can be marked on a birth chart. A birth chart can explain even more about a person than what only a sun sign can. The placement of each planet affects the drive of a person. This reveals personal motivations. Astrology experts can read birth charts.

MAKING CONNECTIONS

TEXT-TO-SELF

Are you a Taurus? If so, do you think the sign matches your personality? If not, what do you have in common with Taureans?

TEXT-TO-TEXT

Have you read any books about the other zodiac signs? How were those signs similar to and different from Taurus?

TEXT-TO-WORLD

With the help of an adult, look up famous Taureans. Pick one person and write a few sentences about ways that person shows Taurus qualities.

GLOSSARY

celestial — having to do with the sky or outer space.

constellation — a group of stars that forms a pattern.

grudge — anger that is held onto for a long time.

internal — of, relating to, or being on the inside.

jealous — wanting what another person has or can do.

luxurious — full of great pleasure and comfort.

motivation — something that makes one want to do something.

represent — to stand for or be a sign of.

spiritual — having to do with people's beliefs in things such as the soul, nature, and what happens after death.

symbol — an object or picture that represents something else.

INDEX

DiscoverRoo!

ONLINE RESOURCES

This book is filled with videos, puzzles, games, and more! Scan the QR codes* while you read, or visit the website below to make this book pop.

popbooksonline.com/taurus

*Scanning QR codes requires a web-enabled smart device with a QR code reader app and a camera.